Inspiration

for a

New Beginning

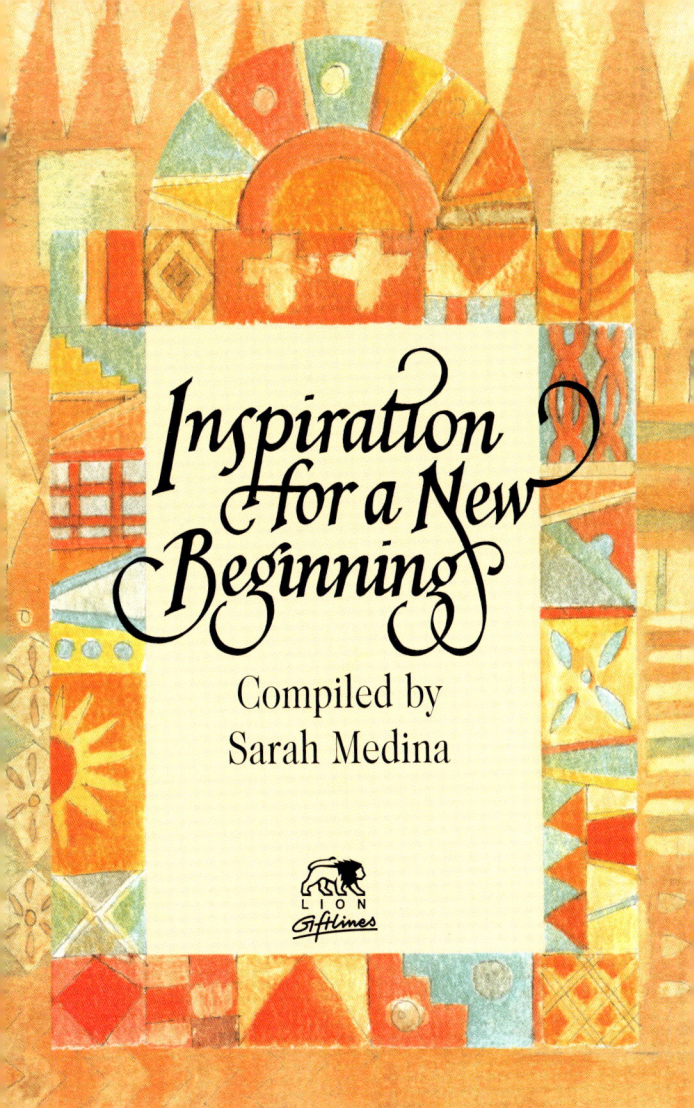

Inspiration for a New Beginning

Compiled by
Sarah Medina

This edition copyright © 1999 Lion Publishing
Illustrations copyright © 1999 Jacqueline Mair
Millennium Resolution copyright © 1999
Churches Together in England

Published by
Lion Publishing plc
Sandy Lane West, Oxford, England
www.lion-publishing.co.uk
ISBN 0 7459 4258 X

First edition 1999
10 9 8 7 6 5 4 3 2 1

All rights reserved

A catalogue record for this book is available
from the British Library

Typeset in 11/13 Caslon 224
Printed and bound in Singapore

Contents

Introduction 6

Respect for the earth 9

Peace for its people 15

Love in our lives 23

Delight in the good 31

Forgiveness for past wrongs 37

A new start 43

INTRODUCTION

There are many occasions when people choose to embrace a 'new beginning'. Birthdays, Christmas, New Year and personal anniversaries of all kinds can offer an opportunity to reflect upon the past, the present and the future.

For some, this is an opportunity – a chance to 'make a fresh start' on a personal level, to make amends with others or to take up a cause to help the wider community. It can bring a sense of excitement and anticipation, a real 'feel-good' factor. Yet for others, the idea of a new start may cause worry and anxiety, like taking a leap into the dark.

There is comfort in knowing that people throughout the world over thousands of years have faced the same issues that are relevant to us today.

What is life all about? Where is it taking me? How can I make things better? Then, as now, individuals and groups have sought to understand and answer these questions.

At the time of a new millennium – the 2,000th anniversary of the birth of Jesus – a wide-ranging group of Christians, represented in the Millennium Group of Churches Together in England, composed a New Year's resolution that could reach out to people all over the world, providing a spiritual focus to the most talked-about 'new beginning' in history.

The words of the Millennium Resolution reflect the eternal concerns of life itself: our world, peace, love, goodness, forgiveness, hope. They are words of comfort and hope for the future.

Alongside them in this compilation, reflecting these themes, you will also discover words from great spiritual writers of the past and present.

May they reach out to you and those you love, bringing hope and inspiration for your new beginning.

Respect for the Earth

There is nothing in creation which does not have some radiance, either greenness or seeds or flowers or beauty – otherwise it would not be part of creation.

HILDEGARD OF BINGEN

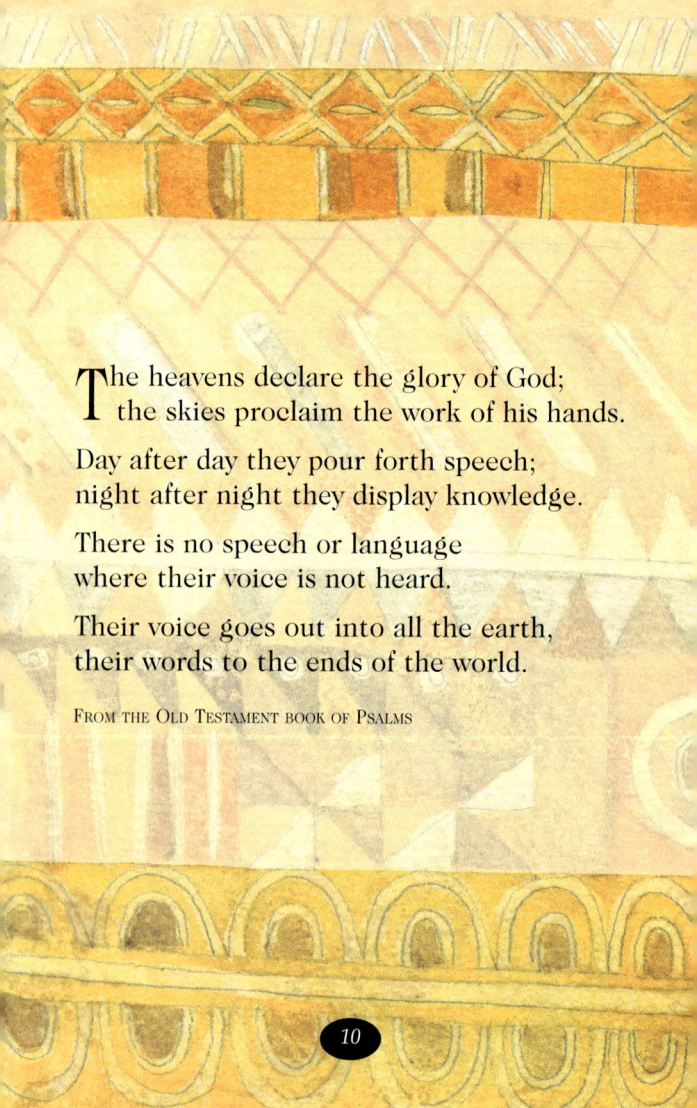

The heavens declare the glory of God;
the skies proclaim the work of his hands.

Day after day they pour forth speech;
night after night they display knowledge.

There is no speech or language
where their voice is not heard.

Their voice goes out into all the earth,
their words to the ends of the world.

From the Old Testament book of Psalms

Love all God's creation, the whole of it and every grain of sand. Love every leaf, every ray of God's light! Love the animals, love the plants, love everything. If you love everything, you will perceive the divine mystery in things. And once you have perceived it, you will begin to comprehend it ceaselessly more and more every day.

FYODOR DOSTOEVSKY

So God created human beings, making them to be like himself. He created them male and female, blessed them, and said, 'Have many children, so that your descendants will live all over the earth and bring it under their control. I am putting you in charge of the fish, the birds, and all the wild animals.'

FROM THE OLD TESTAMENT BOOK OF GENESIS

Enjoy the earth gently
Enjoy the earth gently
For if the earth is spoiled
It cannot be repaired
Enjoy the earth gently.

YORUBA POEM, WEST AFRICA

PEACE FOR ITS PEOPLE

Live in peace yourself
and then you can
bring peace to others.

THOMAS À KEMPIS

Peace between neighbours,
Peace between kindred,
Peace between lovers,
In the love of the King of life.

Peace between person and person,
Peace between wife and husband,
Peace between woman and children,
The peace of Christ above all peace.

From *Carmina Gadelica*

The peace movement is becoming a giant wave in Europe, America and Asia… Voices for peace, coming from the grassroots people in the marginalized areas of the world, have been raised more and more wherever oppression has become dominant… We have to commit ourselves to the world peace movement and give effect to our determination to save succeeding generations from the scourge of war and destruction of our earth.

REIKO SHIMADO

One of the most persistent ambiguities we face is that everybody talks about peace as a goal, but among the wielders of power peace is practically nobody's business. Many men cry 'Peace! Peace!', but they refuse to do the things that make for peace…

One day we must come to see that peace is not merely a distant goal that we seek but a means by which we arrive at that goal. We must pursue peaceful ends through peaceful means. How much longer must we play at deadly war games before we heed the plaintive pleas of the unnumbered dead and maimed of past wars?

MARTIN LUTHER KING JR

The peacemaker's job

The job of the peacemaker is:
  to stop war,
to purify the world,
to get it saved from poverty and riches,
to heal the sick,
to comfort the sad,
to wake up those who have not yet found God,
to create joy and beauty wherever you go,
to find God in everything and in everyone.

MURIEL LESTER

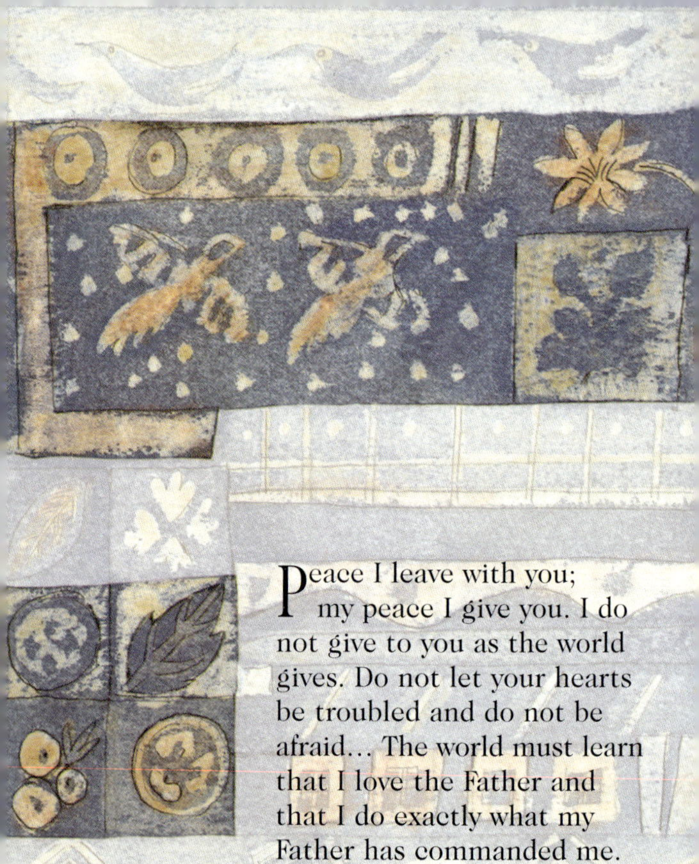

Peace I leave with you;
my peace I give you. I do
not give to you as the world
gives. Do not let your hearts
be troubled and do not be
afraid… The world must learn
that I love the Father and
that I do exactly what my
Father has commanded me.

THE WORDS OF JESUS
IN THE NEW TESTAMENT GOSPEL OF JOHN

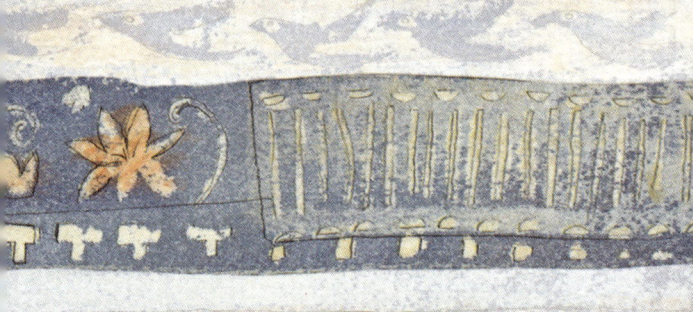

Deep peace of the running wave to you.
Deep peace of the flowing air to you.
Deep peace of the quiet earth to you.
Deep peace of the shining stars to you.
Deep peace of the Son of Peace to you.

CELTIC BLESSING

LOVE IN OUR LIVES

Love alone is capable
of uniting living beings
in such a way as to
complete and fulfil them,
for it alone takes them
and joins them by what
is deepest in themselves.

PIERRE TEILHARD DE CHARDIN

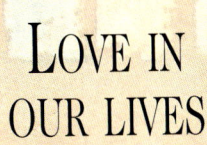

Dear friends, let us love one another, because love comes from God. Whoever loves is a child of God and knows God... And God showed his love for us by sending his only Son into the world, so that we might have life through him... Dear friends, if this is how God loved us, then we should love one another. No one has ever seen God, but if we love one another, God lives in union with us, and his love is made perfect in us.

From the New Testament first letter of John

God is love

A name is not,
cannot, must not be
a label stuck
on persons or on things.

The name comes from within
the things and persons
and must on no account ring false.

It has to express
the essence of the essence,
the real reason
for the being, the existence
of the thing or person named.

Your name
is and only can be
Love.

DOM HELDER CAMARA

I may be able to speak the languages of human beings and even of angels, but if I have no love, my speech is no more than a noisy gong or a clanging bell. I may have the gift of inspired preaching; I may have all knowledge and understand all secrets; I may have all the faith needed to move mountains – but if I have no love, I am nothing. I may give away everything I have, and even give up my body to be burnt – but if I have no love, this does me no good.

    Love is patient and kind; it is not jealous or conceited or proud; love is not ill-mannered or selfish or irritable; love does not keep a record of wrongs; love is not happy with evil, but is happy with the truth. Love never gives up; and its faith, hope and patience never fail.

FROM THE NEW TESTAMENT FIRST LETTER TO THE CORINTHIANS

Joy is love singing
 Peace is love resting
Patience is love enduring
Gentleness is love's character
Faithfulness is love's habit
Meekness is love's self-forgetfulness
Self-control is love holding the reins.

DONALD GREY BARNHOUSE

Love is not a single act, but a climate in which we live, a lifetime venture in which we are always learning, discovering, growing. It is not destroyed by a single failure, or won by a single caress. Love is a climate – a climate of the heart.

ARDIS WHITMAN

Through self-forgetting and self-sacrificing is born a truly creative love. Instead of one emptying the other person for one's own need, each fulfils the other, making him or her more of a person, having more dignity. It brings out the latent qualities in the other, and it partakes somewhat of the love of Christ.

FESTO KIVENGERE

Delight in the Good

To rejoice at another person's joy is like being in heaven.

MEISTER ECKHART

Delight yourself in the Lord and he will give you the desires of your heart.

Commit your way to the Lord; trust in him and he will do this:

He will make your righteousness shine like the dawn,
the justice of your cause like the noonday sun.

FROM THE OLD TESTAMENT BOOK OF PSALMS

Happy are those who know they are spiritually poor;
the Kingdom of heaven belongs to them!

Happy are those who mourn;
God will comfort them!

Happy are those who are humble;
they will receive what God has promised!

Happy are those whose greatest desire is to do what God requires;
God will satisfy them fully!

Happy are those who are merciful to others;
God will be merciful to them!

Happy are the pure in heart;
they will see God!

Happy are those who work for peace;
God will call them his children!

Happy are those who are persecuted because they do what God requires;
the Kingdom of heaven belongs to them!

FROM THE NEW TESTAMENT GOSPEL OF MATTHEW

My God,
I pray that I may so know you and love you
that I may rejoice in you.
And if I may not do so fully in this life
let me go steadily on
to the day when I come to that fullness…
Meanwhile let my mind meditate on it
let my tongue speak of it
let my heart love it
let my mouth preach it
let my soul hunger for it
my flesh thirst for it
and my whole being desire it
until I enter into the joy of my Lord.

St Anselm of Canterbury

Rejoice in the Lord always.
I will say it again: Rejoice!...
Whatever is true,
whatever is noble,
whatever is right,
whatever is pure,
whatever is lovely,
whatever is admirable –
if anything is excellent or
praiseworthy – think about
such things... And the God
of peace will be with you.

From the New Testament letter to the Philippians

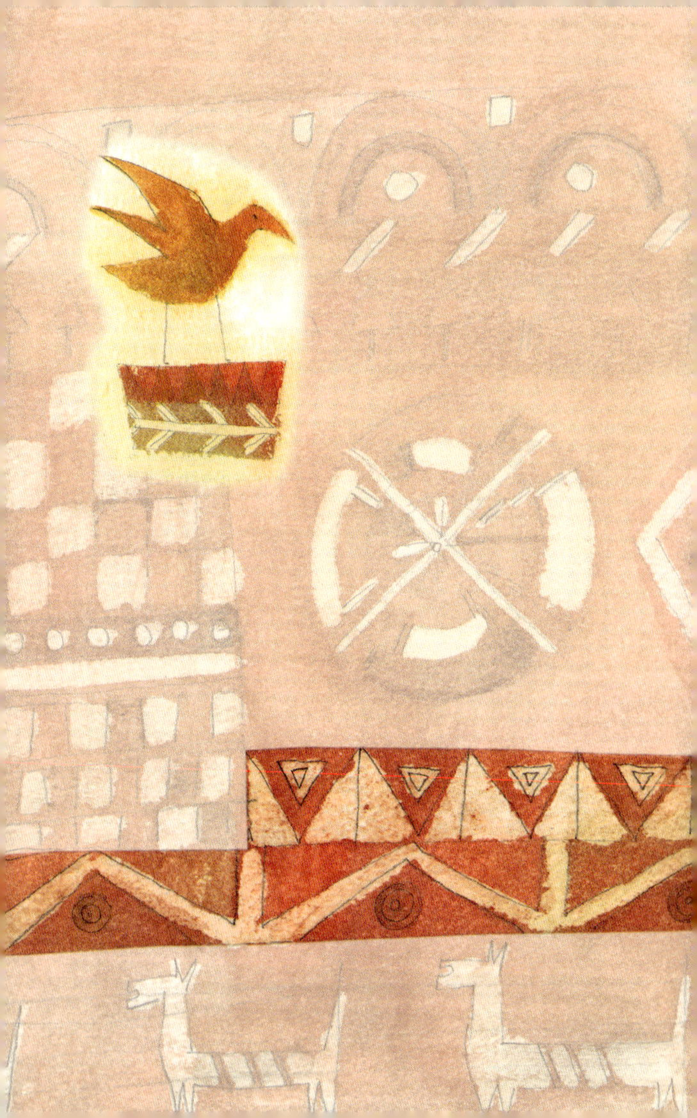

FORGIVENESS FOR PAST WRONGS

Forgiveness is the key that unlocks the door of resentment and the handcuffs of hate. It is a power that breaks the chains of bitterness and the shackles of selfishness.

CORRIE TEN BOOM

The world has never needed more love and forgiveness than it does today. Think of the oppressed countries. There is so much bitterness and hatred as a consequence of what has been suffered. The greatest need is for forgiveness. If they could feel that someone cares about them, that they are loved, perhaps they would find it in their hearts to forgive in their turn. Whatever our belief, we must learn to forgive if we want truly to love. If we remember that we ourselves are sinners and have need of forgiveness, it is easy to forgive others. Unless I have realized this, it is very difficult for me to say, 'I forgive you.' We must make our homes, especially, centres of compassion and forgive endlessly.

Mother Teresa of Calcutta

To be a Christian means to forgive the inexcusable, because God has forgiven the inexcusable in you.

This is hard. It is perhaps not so hard to forgive a single great injury. But to forgive the incessant provocations of daily life – to keep on forgiving the bossy mother-in-law, the bullying husband, the nagging wife, the selfish daughter, the deceitful son – how can we do it? Only, I think, by remembering where we stand, by meaning our words when we say in our prayers each night, 'Forgive us our trespasses as we forgive those that trespass against us.' We are offered forgiveness on no other terms. To refuse it is to refuse God's mercy for ourselves. There is no hint of exceptions and God means what he says.

C.S. LEWIS

Don't be afraid of anything. Do not ever be afraid. And don't worry. So long as you remain sincerely penitent, God will forgive you everything. There's no sin, and there can be no sin in the whole world which God will not forgive to those who are truly repentant. Why, no one can commit so great a sin as to exhaust the infinite love of God. Or can there be a sin that would exceed the love of God?

Fyodor Dostoevsky

There is no other god like you, O Lord;
you forgive the sins of your people…
You do not stay angry for ever, but you take
pleasure in showing us your constant love.
You will be merciful to us once again. You
will trample our sins underfoot and send
them to the bottom of the sea!

FROM THE OLD TESTAMENT BOOK OF MICAH

And from now on...

A NEW START

If you do not hope,
you will not find out what
is beyond your hopes.

St Clement of Alexandria

We wait in hope for the Lord;
he is our help and our shield.

In him our hearts rejoice,
for we trust in his holy name.

May your unfailing love rest upon us, O Lord,
even as we put our hope in you.

FROM THE OLD TESTAMENT BOOK OF PSALMS

It is not the place where you are that is the important thing. It is the intensity of your presence there. It is not the situation that counts. What counts is that you are fully alive in any situation. It is this that puts down roots and then flowers in your life.

NEVILLE CRYER

What a tremendous relief it should be, and has been to many, to discover that we don't need to prove ourselves to God. We don't have to do anything at all, to be acceptable to him. That is what Jesus came to say, and for that he got killed. He came to say, 'Hey, you don't have to earn God's love. It is not a matter for human achievement. You exist because God loves you already. You are a child of divine love.'

DESMOND TUTU

Therefore I tell you, do not worry about your life, what you will eat or drink; or about your body, what you will wear. Is not life more important than food, and the body more important than clothes?…

So do not worry, saying, 'What shall we eat?' or 'What shall we drink?' or 'What shall we wear?' … Your heavenly Father knows that you need them. But seek first his kingdom and his righteousness, and all these things will be given to you as well.

FROM THE NEW TESTAMENT GOSPEL OF MATTHEW

ACKNOWLEDGMENTS

Pages 10, 20, 32, 35, 44, 47: Psalm 19:1–4; John 14:27, 31; Psalm 37:4–6; Philippians 4:4, 8, 9; Psalm 33:20–22; Matthew 6:25, 31, 32–33, quoted from the *Holy Bible, New International Version*, copyright © 1973, 1978, 1984 by International Bible Society. Used by permission.

Pages 12, 24, 26, 33, 41: Genesis 1:27–28; I John 4:7, 9, 11–12; I Corinthians 13:1–7; Matthew 5:3–10; Micah 7:18–19, quoted from the Good News Bible published by The Bible Societies/HarperCollins Publishers Ltd, UK © American Bible Society 1966, 1971, 1976, 1992, used with permission.

Page 16: extract taken from *Carmina Gadelica* by Alexander Carmichael, copyright © 1992, 1994 Floris Books. Used by permission of Scottish Academic Press.

Page 19: extract quoted in *Baptist Peacemaker* (spring/summer 1995).

Page 25: extract taken from *Into Your Hands* by Dom Helder Camara, published and copyright © 1987 by Darton Longman and Todd Ltd and used by permission of the publishers.

Page 46: extract taken from *Hope and Suffering* by Desmond Tutu, reproduced by permission of HarperCollins Publishers Ltd.

We would like to thank all those who have given us permission to include material in this book. Every effort has been made to trace and acknowledge copyright holders of all the quotations in this book. We apologize for any errors or omissions that may remain, and would ask those concerned to contact the publishers, who will ensure that full acknowledgment is made in the future.